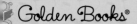

READING ON YOUR OWN

MILE
3

ROAD TO READING

ALLIGATORS

Life in the Wild

D0096716

by Monica Kulling
illustrated by Marty Roper

ROAD TO READING

DRIVER'S LICENSE
ID #333-333-333

Name
_____

Date
_____

Signature
_____

USA $3.99/CAN $4.99
ITEM: 26325-00
ISBN 0-307-26325-8

9 780307 263254

50399

Dear Parent:

Buckle up! You are about to join your child on a very exciting journey. The destination? Independent reading!

Road to Reading will help you and your child get there. The program offers books at five levels, or Miles, that accompany children from their first attempts at reading to successfully reading on their own. Each Mile is paved with engaging stories and delightful artwork.

Getting Started
For children who know the alphabet and are eager to begin reading
• easy words • fun rhythms • big type • picture clues

Reading With Help
For children who recognize some words and sound out others with help
• short sentences • pattern stories • simple plotlines

Reading On Your Own
For children who are ready to read easy stories by themselves
• longer sentences • more complex plotlines • easy dialogue

First Chapter Books
For children who want to take the plunge into chapter books
• bite-size chapters • short paragraphs • full-color art

Chapter Books
For children who are comfortable reading independently
• longer chapters • occasional black-and-white illustrations

There's no need to hurry through the Miles. Road to Reading is designed without age or grade levels. Children can progress at their own speed, developing confidence and pride in their reading ability no matter what their age or grade.

So sit back and enjoy the ride—every Mile of the way!

For Lori Haskins,
editor par excellence

M.K.

To my sons, Aaron and Noah, whose interest in
exotic creatures rivals my own

M.R.

Thanks to Dr. Ruth M. Elsey of the Louisiana Department of
Wildlife and Fisheries/Rockefeller Wildlife Refuge for all her
help with this book.

Library of Congress Cataloging-in-Publication Data
Kulling, Monica.
Alligators : life in the wild / by Monica Kulling ; illustrated by Marty Roper.
  p.   cm. — (Road to reading. Mile 3)
Summary: Describes the physical characteristics, hunting and
feeding behavior, habitat, life cycle, and methods of communication of alligators.
ISBN 0-307-26325-8 (pbk) — ISBN 0-307-46325-7 (GB)
1. Alligators—Juvenile literature.   [1. Alligators.]
I. Roper, Marty, ill.   II. Title.   III. Series.
QL666.C925K85   1999
597.98—dc21

                                        98-29323
                                        CIP
                                        AC

A GOLDEN BOOK • New York
Golden Books Publishing Company, Inc. New York, New York 10106

ISBN: 0-307-26325-8 (pbk)   A MM
ISBN: 0-307-46325-7 (GB)

ALLIGATORS

Life in the Wild

by MONICA KULLING
illustrated by MARTY ROPER

It is early morning
in the Florida Everglades.
The swamp is quiet and still.
Two eyes peer
above the murky water.
They belong to an alligator—
a hungry alligator.

A heron lands nearby.

WHOOSH!

The alligator bursts

out of the water.

The heron tries to take off,

but the alligator is too fast.

SNAP!

The alligator's sharp teeth

close on the heron.

There is no escape.

Alligators are mighty hunters.
They are among
the oldest hunters, or *predators*,
on Earth.

They have been around
for nearly sixty-five million years—
since dinosaur times!

There are two species of alligators.
The Chinese alligator
can be found
in the Yangtze River in China.

The American alligator

lives in the southeastern United States.

Florida, Texas, and Louisiana

are some of the states

where the American alligator

makes its home.

11

Alligators look almost the same
as they did millions of years ago.
Their skin is made of hard scales.
These scales are as tough as armor,
but they move and bend easily.
Alligators have powerful tails,
huge, strong jaws,
and seventy sharp teeth!

Alligators do not use
their teeth for chewing.
Instead, they use them for tearing.

An alligator tears its prey
into pieces by twisting it
around and around underwater.
Then the alligator swallows
the pieces whole.

Some alligators have stones
in their stomachs!
The stones grind up
the alligator's food
so it is easier to digest.
The stones have another use, too.
They help keep the alligator
underwater!

Alligators can stay underwater
for hours at a time.
Their nostrils shut tight
to keep water out.
Thin flaps of skin cover their ears.
And special, clear eyelids
protect their eyes.

Alligators spend most of
their time in the water.
But they need the land, too.
That's because alligators are *reptiles*.

Reptiles are cold-blooded animals.
This means that the temperature
of their bodies matches
the temperature around them.
When the water gets cold,
alligators get cold, too.
So they crawl out on land
to warm up in the sun.

Alligators also need the land
for another reason—
to lay their eggs.
This female alligator
is building a nest
of mud and plants.
When she is done,
she will dig a hole in the nest
and lay her eggs inside.

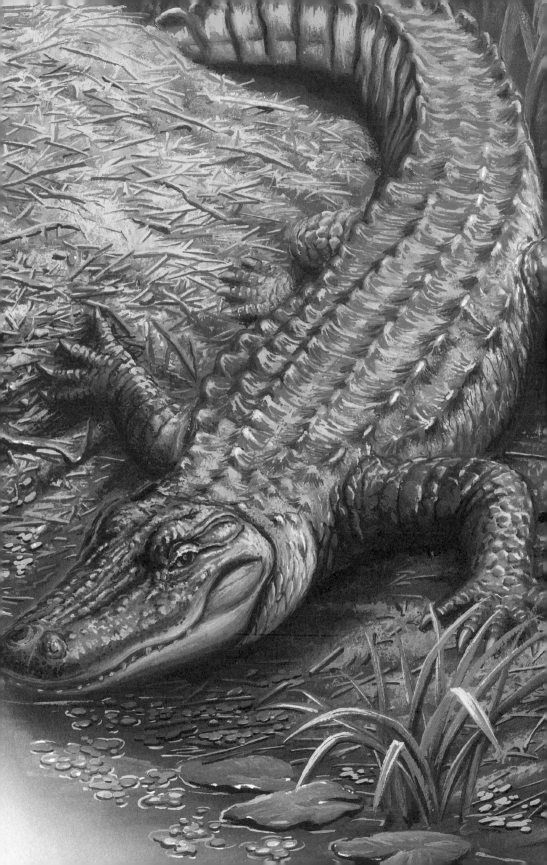

An alligator can lay
up to forty eggs at a time!
Each egg is a little bit larger
than a hen's egg.

The mother alligator
covers the eggs
with mud and plants
to keep them warm.
Then she lies down nearby
to guard the nest.

The mother alligator watches
her nest day and night.
When she sees
a hungry raccoon come near,
she races over to protect her eggs.
The raccoon leaves—fast!

Ten weeks pass.

The eggs begin to hatch.

Inside their hard shells,

the hatchlings yelp and croak.

The mother alligator hears
the hatchlings' cries.
Quickly, she digs up the eggs.

One of the hatchlings
can't break its shell!
The mother alligator
picks up the egg.
She rolls it gently
against the roof of her mouth
with her tongue.

The shell breaks,
and the mother alligator
sets the hatchling
safely on the ground.

Mother alligators take good care
of their young.
Here, the mother lets
the hatchlings lie on her head
to catch some sun!

Meanwhile,
she is keeping a close eye
on a hawk in a nearby tree.
Hawks, raccoons, and black snakes
all like to eat baby alligators.
But they won't have a chance—
not if the mother alligator
can help it.

Grown alligators
watch out for each other, too.
Sometimes they share food.
When there is a dry spell,
they share what little water
they can find.

Alligators even "talk"
to each other!
They roar, or *bellow*,
messages back and forth.

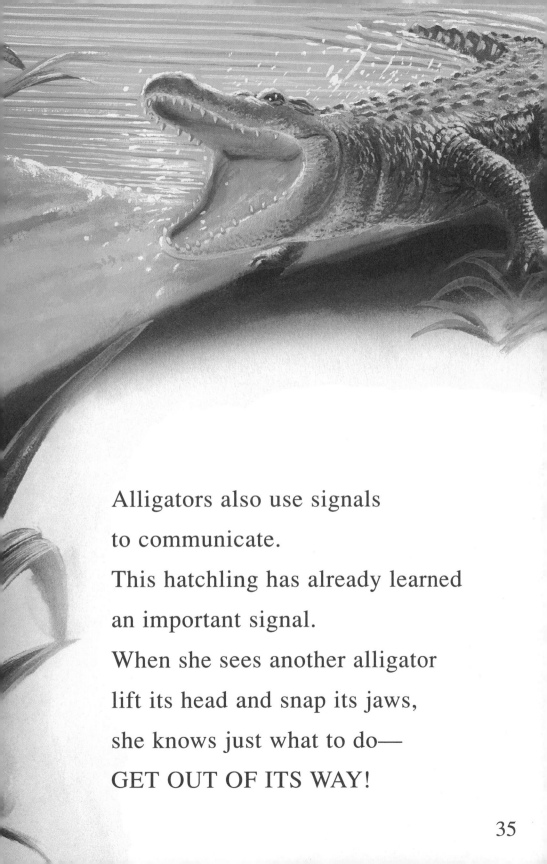

Alligators also use signals
to communicate.
This hatchling has already learned
an important signal.
When she sees another alligator
lift its head and snap its jaws,
she knows just what to do—
GET OUT OF ITS WAY!

The hatchlings grow quickly—
about a foot a year!
At first they eat mostly bugs.
Soon birds, frogs, and turtles
are on the menu.

By age six, the hatchlings are adults.

But they don't stop growing.

Adult alligators grow

a little bit every day

for the rest of their lives.

A male alligator can grow to be
fourteen feet long—
as long as a station wagon!

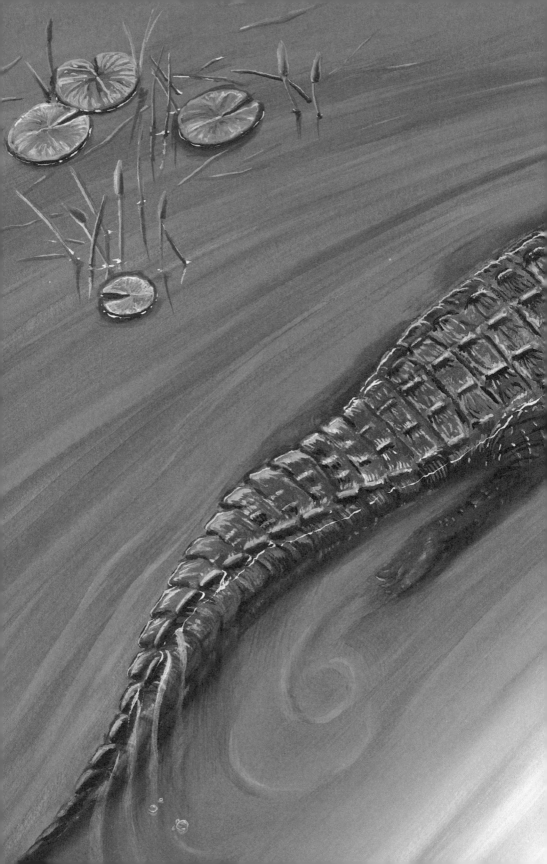

Alligators are strong swimmers.
When an alligator swims,
it folds its legs against its body
so it is shaped like a fish.
Then the alligator sweeps its tail
back and forth in the water.

When an alligator wants to swim fast,
it whips its tail hard.

At top speed, an alligator
sometimes rises out of the water.
It looks as if it's walking on its tail!

Alligators are fast and fierce.
They can catch
just about any animal
that comes near the water.
This alligator is about to catch a deer
that was drinking at the river's edge.

After this feast, the alligator
will not need to eat again
for a long time.
An adult alligator can survive
on one big meal for a whole year!

Are alligators dangerous to people?

They can be.

If they are *provoked*, or bothered,

alligators will attack humans.

People can be dangerous
to alligators, too.
Many of the swamps and marshes
where alligators live
are being drained away
to make room for houses or businesses.
Every year there is less and less space
for alligators.

It's important to preserve
the alligator's home.
If we do, this creature
that has been on Earth
for millions of years
will survive for many, many more.